HANDMADE
PUZZLES IN WOOD

Dedication

I dedicate this book to the readers and friends who transformed hesitation into progress on this lonely journey with their warm support and encouragement.

Handmade Puzzles in Wood is an original work, first published in 2024 by Fox Chapel Publishing Company, Inc. The patterns contained herein are copyrighted by the author. Readers may make copies of these patterns for personal use. The patterns themselves, however, are not to be duplicated for resale or distribution under any circumstances. Any such copying is a violation of copyright law.

ISBN: 978-1-4971-0478-5

The Cataloging-in-Publication Data is on file with the Library of Congress.

Managing Editor: Gretchen Bacon
Acquisitions Editor: Kaylee J. Schofield
Editor: Joseph Borden
Designer: Matthew Hartsock
Proofreader: Kelly Umenhofer
Photography by Mike Mihalo

To learn more about the other great books from Fox Chapel Publishing, or to find a retailer near you, call toll-free 800-457-9112, send mail to 903 Square Street, Mount Joy, PA 17552, or visit us at *www.FoxChapelPublishing.com*.

We are always looking for talented authors. To submit an idea, please send a brief inquiry to acquisitions@foxchapelpublishing.com.

Printed in China
First printing

HANDMADE
PUZZLES IN WOOD

Making Interlocking Treasures—with 200+ Ready-to-Use Patterns

FOX CHAPEL
PUBLISHING

JAEHEON YUN

Table of Contents

Introduction

For quite long time, I've been designing only animal puzzles, but I didn't have the flexibility to try anything other than that. New attempts and creations often seem to begin unintentionally, often sparked by whimsical imagination.

I always thought adding a narrative to puzzles would make them more enjoyable. The interpretation of scenes in this book offers a diverse and intriguing storyline different from traditional puzzles. At first, starting with one or two puzzles, I was not sure what I should depict. However, as I progressed, I discovered that making puzzles around scene topics is genuinely fascinating and enjoyable.

In this book, there are truly diverse stories hidden within. It includes tales about insects, as well as myths, religion, and interesting compositions expressed solely through objects.

In these pages, I've told the stories I set out to tell. I can't wait to see what stories you'll create!

About the Author

Jaeheon Yun is a puzzle designer based in South Korea. He graduated from Seowon University with a degree in Industrial Design in 2004; then, just before his first child was born in 2011, he bought a scroll saw and began making toys. Find more of his work on Etsy at Namunolie.

About the Test Cutter

Rolf Beuttenmuller started scrolling in 2004 after his wife, June, bought him a scroll saw for his birthday. He joined a local club and enjoys new and challenging projects. His motto is, "I don't know that I can't, therefore I can." Rolf retired from Brookhaven National Lab after 34 years of designing and building special devices for high energy and photon science research. He lives in Bellport, N.Y.

Getting Started

If you're new to scroll saw woodworking, the projects in this book are perfect for you. Each is designed to be approachable and adaptable to your skill level. If a project is too small and difficult for you to cut, make it bigger. If the pieces don't come out just as you'd expected, adapt them so they'll work. The only limit is your imagination! Before you get started, though, let's go over some basic tool and safety considerations.

I HAVE A FEW MORE TIPS TO SHARE BEFORE YOU GET STARTED:

- If you are using a sturdy hardwood for a puzzle, try making the animals' tails and horns (if any) a little longer.

- If you have a good piece of wood, but it's smaller than the pattern, omit the animals on the far left, right, and on top. No one will know!

- If you cut with the wood grain in mind, your puzzle pieces will be stronger. Pieces like tails, mouths, and ears could break more easily if they do not run in the direction of the grain.

- If your wood looks nice but the grain is weak, omit the small details (nose, mouth, extra lines, etc.). The beauty of the wood will make up for these details in the overall look of the project.

- Make a colorful puzzle by using several pieces of wood in different colors (e.g., walnut, cherry, soft maple, beech, various exotic woods).

- If you'd like to make a smaller puzzle, either reduce the number of animals or reduce the size of the pattern by 10 – 30%.

- If you start to veer away from the pattern line while cutting, come back to the line slowly. Think of these deviations as an opportunity to create more natural-looking lines.

- If the puzzles will be used by small children, I recommend softening the sharp corners with a sander after cutting.

Note: While the notes on each project indicate the type of wood and finish used in the completed puzzle pictured, scrollers can use whatever materials they prefer.

Meet the Scroll Saw

A scroll saw is an electrically powered saw with a reciprocating blade that moves up and down to cut through wood and other materials. One of the main advantages of a scroll saw is its removable blade, which you can easily insert into a predrilled hole and cut outward from the center of your project. Thanks to the scroll saw's versatility and ability to handle curves, tight corners, and tricky cuts, it is an excellent choice for creating beginner-friendly puzzles like those in this book. Since the blade and saw are fixed, your job is to move the workpiece around, rather than moving the tool in relation to the workpiece. You're in control! Remember: go slow, have fun, and let the blade do the work.

AUTHOR'S NOTE:

These projects look great in various sizes. If you choose to make them smaller or larger, be sure to adjust the drill bit sizes for the eyes and other features accordingly.

Materials and Tools

Only a few tools are needed to complete every project in this book—and they're probably already lying around your shop! You'll need a scroll saw and blades, your choice of wood, a sander for preparing blanks, clamps, and a drill press and bits.

Other Useful Items

- **Acrylic paints and stains:** I chose to distinguish my puzzle pieces from one another with contrasting wood varieties and stains, but you can add pops of color with acrylic paints, if desired.
- **Air compressor or tack cloth:** To blow away excess dust.
- **Blue painter's tape, removeable shelf liner, scroller's tape, temporary-bond spray adhesive, graphite or carbon transfer paper:** For attaching patterns to wood. Alternatively, use rubber cement or glue sticks instead of spray adhesive.
- **Food-safe finish:** For puzzles or toys a child will come in contact with, I prefer Danish oil or mineral oil, but you can use a food-safe finish of your choice.
- **Mineral spirits or commercial adhesive removers:** To aid in removing paper patterns from wood.
- **Pencil or red pen:** To mark measurements or trace patterns as needed.
- **Rotary tool with bits:** To round over sharp edges on a puzzle.
- **Sandpaper:** For smoothing pieces of wood before and after scrolling.

80 grit   120 grit   300 grit

SANDING THROUGH THE GRITS

The grit number on a length of sandpaper refers to the average number of particles per square inch. The lower numbers, such as 60 and 80, are the coarser grits, which remove the most wood and are used for rough shaping. The higher numbers—220 and above—refer to finer grits that remove less wood and are used for smoothing. "Sanding through the grits" simply means using progressively finer sandpapers to smooth the scratches left by coarser grits. Rub sandpaper on a project until the wood is smooth and shaped the way you want, then move on to a finer grit of paper and repeat, sanding with the grain when possible.

Safety

Take the time to properly prepare your workspace so that your scrolling experience is safe and enjoyable. Work in a well-ventilated space and surround your setup with good, even lighting. Always wear a dust mask and safety goggles, tie up long hair, and secure loose clothing before beginning a project in your shop. When using power tools, such as drum sanders and band saws, employ a benchtop dust collector to help keep your work area clean and protect your lungs to ensure that you can scroll without difficulty for years to come.

Choosing Wood

Each project is presented with a list of wood and drill bit dimensions, as well as a recommendation on which wood and finish to use. Here, I've listed some common wood varieties you may find useful.

Cherry: This hardwood has a rich, reddish hue and is similar to walnut in hardness. Cherry burns easily when cut with a  power saw, so make sure to cover the wood with clear packaging tape before applying the pattern. In addition, you could use a large skip-tooth blade, as this can reduce the amount of dust that gets caught in the kerf (the cut path created by a blade).

Maple: Dense and light in color with a distinctive grain, maple is highly prized by woodworkers. Just make sure to apply clear  packaging tape to the surface of the wood before attaching a pattern, as maple can burn easily.

Pine: Light-colored and beloved for its affordability and ubiquity, pine is a great starter wood for beginners to scrolling.

Poplar: Soft and easy to work with, poplar often takes on a slight greenish tinge once a finish is applied.

Walnut: This durable wood is prized for its workability and deep, chocolatey color.

WHY IS WOOD DUST A HEALTH CONCERN?

Wood dust is considered carcinogenic to humans. Exposure to certain kinds of wood dust has been associated with health issues due to the natural chemicals in the wood, or substances in the wood such as bacteria, mold, and fungi. Wood dust is also associated with toxic effects; irritation of the eyes, nose, and throat dermatitis; and respiratory system effects, including decreased lung capacity and allergic reactions. It is imperative to wear personal protective equipment (see Safety above) while working with wood. Always research a wood's toxicity before beginning any project.

Selecting a Blade

Not only do blades come in different sizes, but the cutting teeth come in different configurations and different numbers of teeth per inch (TPI). As a general rule, the thickness of a blade increases as the numbers ascend; for instance, a #3 blade will have a smaller kerf than a #7 blade and be better suited to detail work, or thinner pieces of wood. You'll use two main blade types for the projects in this book:

SKIP-TOOTH

Skip-tooth blades are the most common configuration. Instead of having one tooth right next to the last, they skip one tooth, leaving an open space between the teeth. The space helps clear sawdust and helps the blade cut faster. Skip-tooth blades produce a slightly rougher cut surface, so you will likely need to sand after cutting.

Note: This chart can be used for both blade types pictured.

REVERSE-TOOTH

Reverse-tooth blades usually follow the skip-tooth configuration, but with the bottom couple of teeth pointed in the opposite direction from the rest. These teeth cut as the saw blade travels upward. Where the skip-tooth, double-tooth, and regular-tooth blades splinter the bottom of the blank slightly, reverse-tooth blades remove these splinters. Reverse-tooth blades produce a cleaner bottom cut than other blades, but they don't clear as much sawdust. The sawdust can slow the cutting and possibly heat the blade, making it more likely to break or scorch the wood.

WOOD	THICKNESS	BLADE SIZE
Hardwood, softwood, plywood	¼" (6mm) or thinner	#2/0 to #1
Hardwood, softwood, plywood	¼" to ½" (6mm to 1.3cm)	#1 to #2
Hardwood, softwood, plywood	½" to ¾" (1.3cm to 1.9cm)	#3 to #4
Hardwood (less dense), softwood, plywood	¾" to 1" (1.9cm to 2.5cm)	#4 to #6
Hardwood (dense)	¾" to 1" (1.9cm to 2.5cm)	#5 to #7

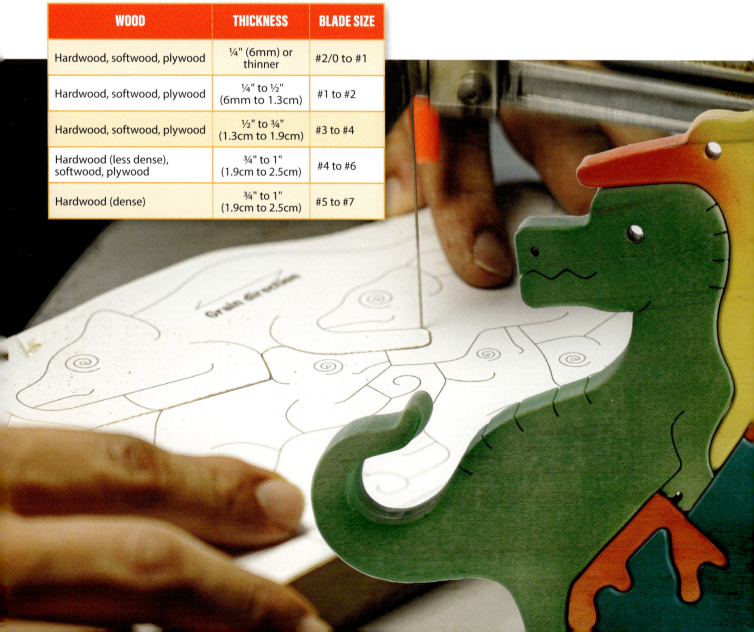

Choosing a Finish

You can finish the projects in this book in a number of ways; I've included suggestions here. I recommend a food-safe finish, especially if the puzzles will be handled by young children. Most finishes are food-safe when fully cured; however, always read the manufacturer's instructions thoroughly before applying a finish to any project. *Note: Be sure to dispose of oil-soaked rags properly and according to the manufacturer's instructions, as they can spontaneously combust.*

Acrylic Paints, Stains, and Dyes

Apply color to your projects with transparent stains or washes of water-based acrylics. The benefit of a transparent stain or paint wash is that it allows the attractive wood grain to remain visible. You could also choose to use glossy paints because they eliminate a finishing step by acting as their own topcoat.

Food-Safe Finishes

Carnauba wax: Derived from the Brazilian palm tree, this wax is harder and more water-resistant than beeswax. Used as a light protective coating or topcoat polish, carnauba wax is a popular choice for woodworkers.

Danish oil: Highly versatile, water resistant, and food-safe when fully cured, natural Danish oil is a popular choice for puzzles. It dries to a hard, satin finish and will darken the wood

slightly. It can be combined with oil-based pigments to create wood stains.

Mixture of mineral oil and beeswax: Easily whipped up and applied, this mixture ensures the longevity of your puzzles. The simple mixture not only restores and protects but also leaves your items with a light scent of honey.

Raw linseed oil: Not to be confused with boiled linseed oil (which can contain toxic additives), this simple, flaxseed-derived oil is hard-wearing, water-resistant, and suitable for use on hard or close-grained wood.

Shellac: Harvested from a bug in India, shellac is a versatile, nontoxic wood finish that enhances the natural grain while adding smoothness without the plastic-like qualities of polyurethane or lacquer.

Tung oil: Extracted from nuts, tung oil often requires numerous coats. It leaves a natural finish that darkens the wood while showcasing the grain. Once thoroughly cured, it is food-safe.

Clear Finishes

Clear spray or brush-on finishes provide a final sealing coat that boosts resistance to chipping and moisture without obscuring the wood grain. Acrylic, lacquer, or polyurethane sprays typically come in several varieties, ranging from matte to gloss.

Making the Puzzles: Step-by-Step Guide

Each of the projects in this book can be made using the following process. Modify the size, wood type, and finishing method as desired. You can even cut the pieces of one puzzle from a variety of contrasting hardwoods for added interest.

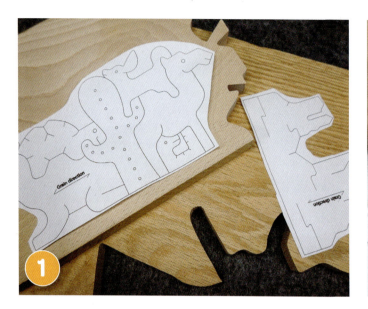

Prepare the blank for cutting. I recommend an orbital sander, but you could sand by hand if desired. Cover the blank with removable shelf liner or painter's tape. Then, photocopy the pattern and adhere it to the surface. *Note: You could also apply the pattern directly to the wood with repositionable adhesive.*

Cut the profiles of the pieces on a scroll saw. Blade size and type will depend on the variety and thickness of the wood used. I do not recommend spiral blades, as the wide kerf could mangle some of the fine details.

Clamp each piece securely in a drill press. Then drill any holes needed (eyes, nostrils, etc.), following the bit size guides on the patterns. Return to the scroll saw and cut the fine kerf details on the pieces.

Carefully remove the patterns. Take care not to scratch the wood with your fingernails.

Sand the fronts and backs of the pieces to remove fuzzies. I used an orbital sander.

Sand the edges of the pieces. I used a small spindle sander.

Refine the edges. I used a rotary tool with a cone-shaped sanding drum to fit into the tight areas. Soften the sharp corners, and then give the pieces a final sand to 320 grit by hand. Remove dust with a tack cloth.

Apply a finish. Be sure to use protective gloves.

Gallery

Arctic Adventure (page 39)

Fantastic Frenzy (page 59)

Dino Volcano (page 37)

Dino Volcano (page 37)

You can paint your puzzle pieces whatever colors you'd like!

Dragons' Keep (page 29)

Desert Mirage (page 22)

Dino Volcano (page 37)

Hooves and Feathers (page 35)

Sunshine Savannah (page 25)

Projects

Desert Mirage

Desert Mirage: 7 pieces

Size: 12¹⁵⁄₁₆" x 4⁵⁄₁₆" (328 x 110mm)

Eye size: ¹⁄₁₆" (2mm), ⅛" (3mm)

Recommended wood: ¾" (19mm) hard maple

Camel and tortoise pals share a sandy stroll in this easy-to-assemble puzzle. Join their desert walk and bring the adventure to life, one piece at a time!

Desert Mirage Pattern (Animals)

Photocopy at 100%

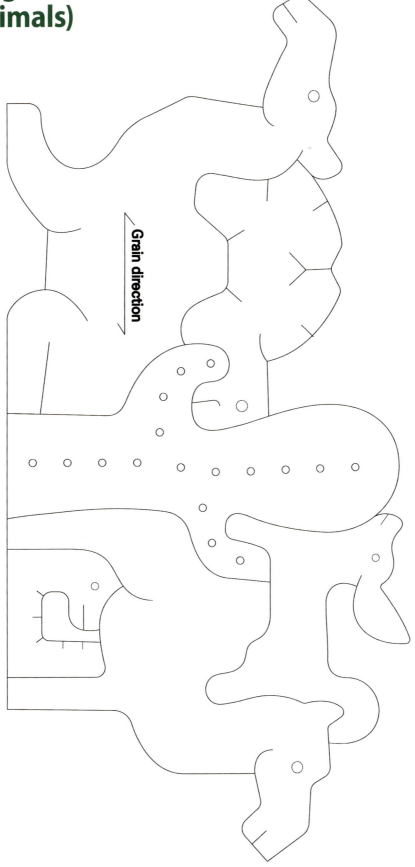

Grain direction

Desert Mirage
Pattern (Landscape)

Photocopy at 100%

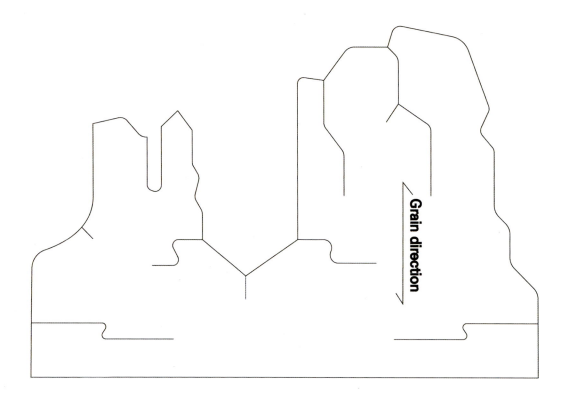

Grain direction

Sunshine Savannah

Sunshine Savannah: 9 pieces

Size: 10¾" x 7⅜" (272.7 x 188mm)

Eye size: ¹⁄₁₆" (2mm), ⅛" (3mm), ⁵⁄₃₂" (4mm)

Recommended wood: ¾" (19mm) walnut

Build your own safari with this wooden puzzle, where a tall giraffe and a mighty elephant find shade under a lush tree. It's a wild world in miniature, just waiting for your touch to come alive.

Sunshine Savannah
Pattern

Photocopy at 125%

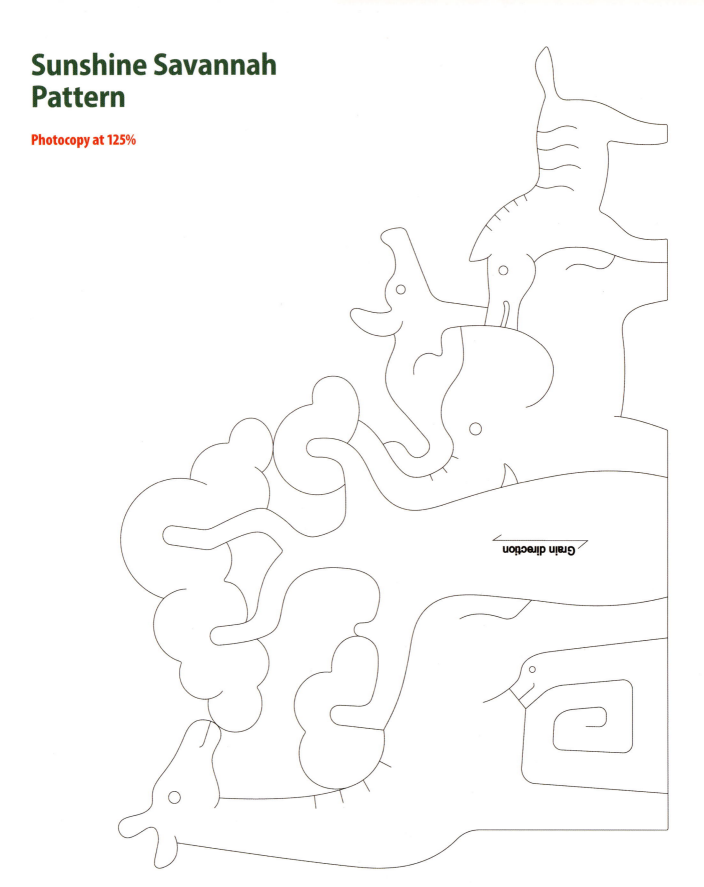

Grain direction

Farmyard Friends

Farmyard Friends: 10 pieces

Size: 9¾" x 7½" (247 x 190mm)

Eye size: ⅛" (3mm), ⁵⁄₃₂" (4mm)

Nose Size: ¹⁄₃₂" (1mm), ¹⁄₁₆" (2mm)

Recommended wood: ¾" (19mm) walnut

Craft this farmyard puzzle to discover a tree where piglets play hide-and-seek with friendly cows. It's a charming countryside scene that's sure to bring a smile with every piece.

Farmyard Friends Pattern

Photocopy at 100%

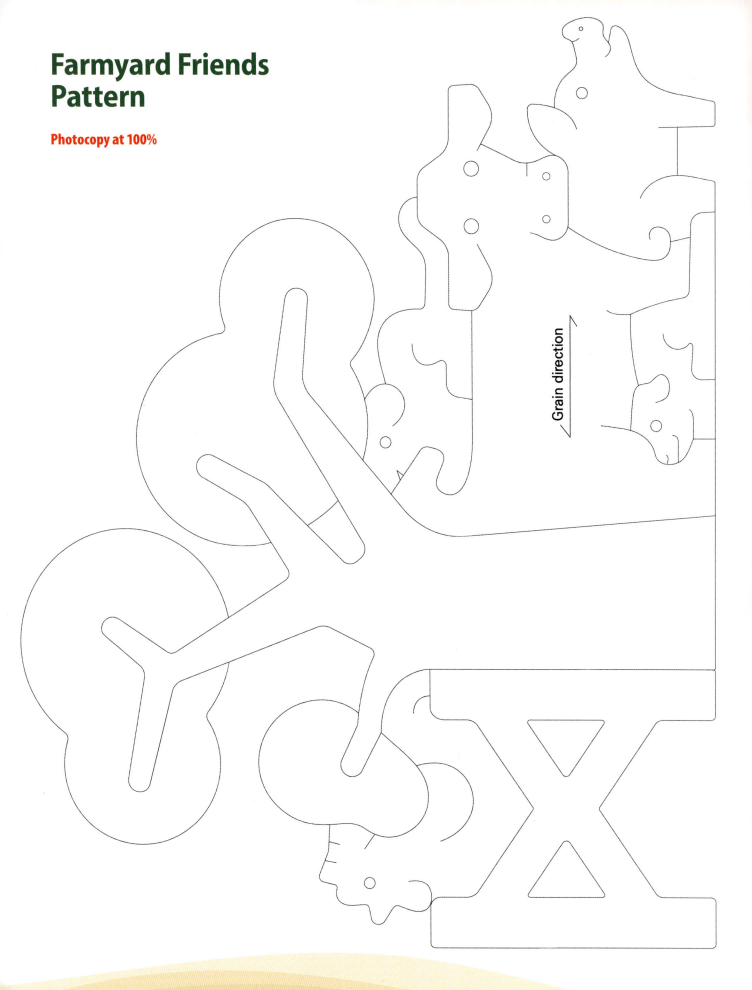

Grain direction

Dragons' Keep

Dragons' Keep: 4 pieces

Size: 14¼" x 5⁵⁄₁₆" (362 x 135mm)

Eye size: ⁵⁄₃₂" (4mm)

Castle window hole size: ⁵⁄₃₂" (4mm)

Recommended wood: ¾" (19mm) hard maple

Create your own fantasy castle with dragons as guards in this magical wooden puzzle. Every piece adds to the enchantment!

Dragons' Keep
Pattern (Part A)

Photocopy at 100%

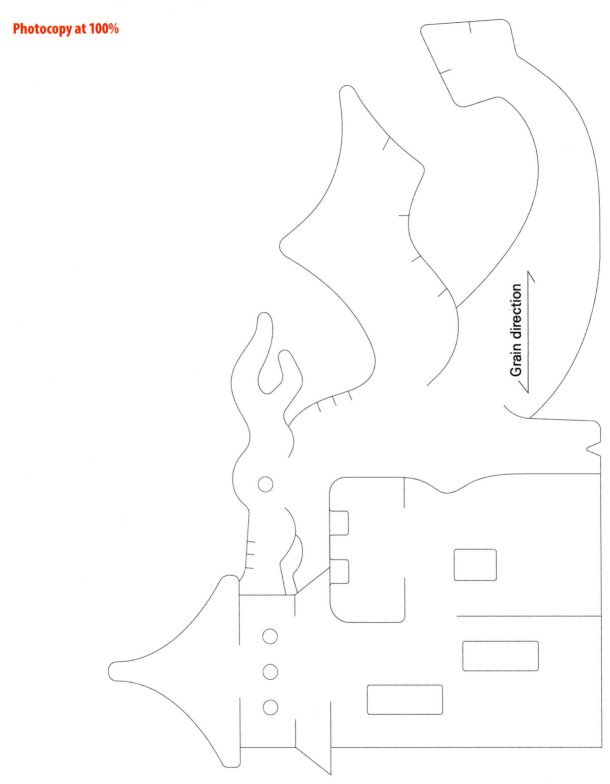

Grain direction

Dragons' Keep
Pattern (Part B)

Photocopy at 100%

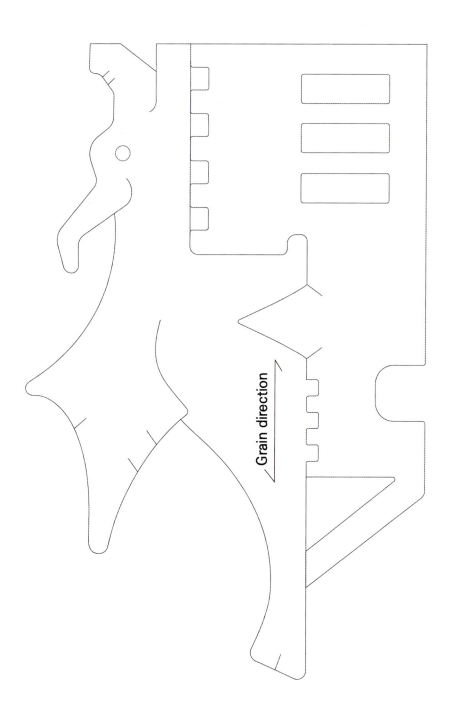

Grain direction

Dragon Siege

Storm the castle with this knightly wooden puzzle, where noble steeds and brave warriors are ready for action. Add personal touches to tell your own magical tale.

Dragon Siege: 9 pieces

Size: 14⅞" x 5⅛" (377.5 x 130mm)

Eye size: human, 1/16" (1.5mm); dragon, 5/32" (4mm)

Castle window hole size: 3/16" (5mm)

Recommended wood: ¾" (19mm) hard maple

Dragon Siege
Pattern (Part A)

Photocopy at 125%

Grain direction

Dragon Siege
Pattern (Part B)

Photocopy at 100%

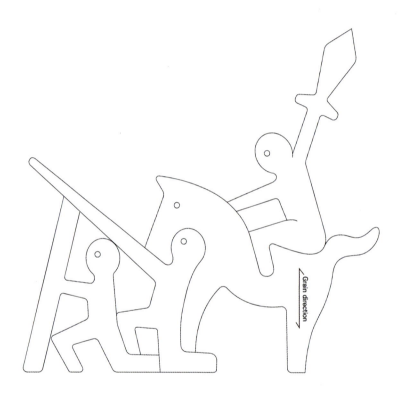

Grain direction

Hooves and Feathers

Hooves and Feathers: 18 pieces

Size: 8¼" x 7 11/16" (210 x 195mm)

Horse eye size: ⅛" (3mm)

Bird eye size: 1/16" (2mm)

Recommended wood: ¾" (19mm) hard maple

Perched birds and prancing horses come together in this charming tree-filled scene. See how many pieces you can balance on the branches before they all come tumbling down!

Hooves and Feathers
Pattern

Photocopy at 125%

Grain direction

Dino Volcano

Dino Volcano: 8 pieces
Size: 10⅞" x 5¹¹⁄₁₆" (276 x 145mm)
Eye size: ⅛" (3mm)
Nose size: ¹⁄₁₆" (1.5mm)
Recommended wood: ¾" (19mm) hard maple

Roaring dinosaurs gather around a fiery volcano in this vibrant wooden puzzle. Bring this prehistoric scene to life and imagine the thunderous sounds of a land lost in time.

Dino Volcano
Pattern

Photocopy at 125%

Grain direction

Arctic Adventure

Arctic Adventure: 8 pieces

Size: 10⅞" x 5¹¹⁄₁₆" (276 x 145mm)

Eye size: ⅛" (3mm)

Nose size: ¹⁄₁₆" (1.5mm)

Recommended wood: ¾" (19mm) hard maple

Slide into a cool world with penguins, polar bears, and a seal, all playing on icy peaks. This frosty wooden puzzle captures the playful spirit of Arctic friends.

Arctic Adventure
Pattern

Photocopy at 100%

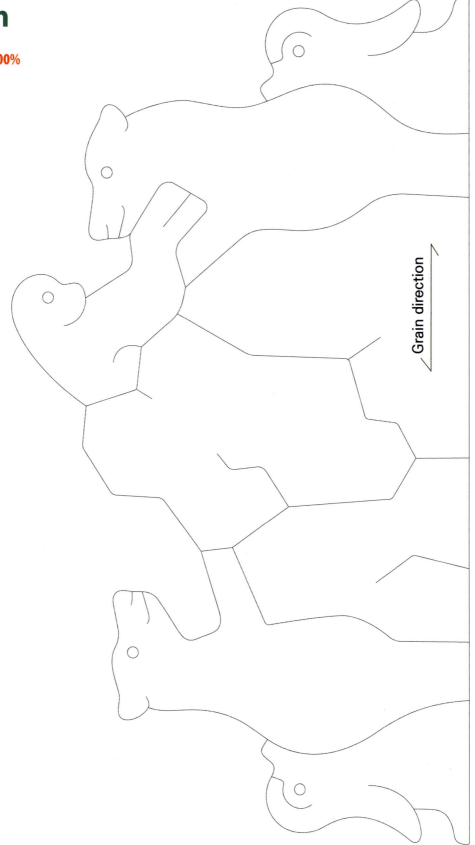

Grain direction

A Fish Tale

A Fish Tale: 9 pieces

Size: 11" x 5½" (280 x 140mm)

Eye size: ¹⁄₁₆" (2mm)

Recommended wood: ¾" (19mm) hard maple

This peaceful puzzle is a nature-lover's dream! Cut a bunch and gift them to all the outdoor enthusiasts in your life. When cutting, take extra care around the fishing pole, as it's more delicate.

A Fish Tale
Pattern

Photocopy at 125%

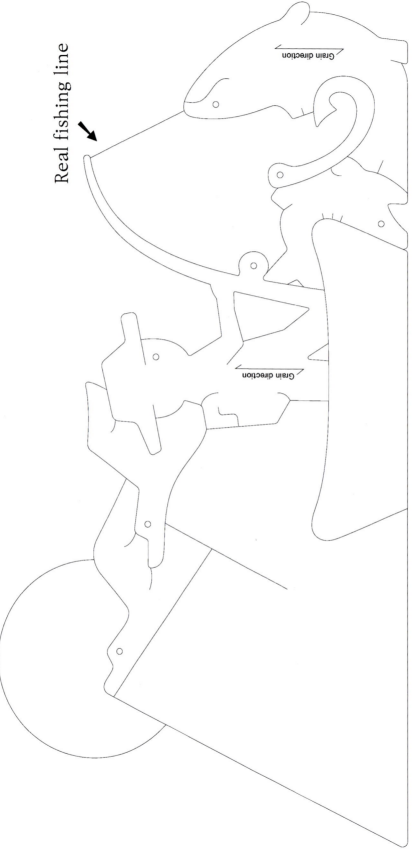

Jungle Canopy

Jungle Canopy: 12 pieces

Size: 9⅝" x 7½" (244.5 x 190mm)

Eye size: TK

Leaf hole: ¹⁄₁₆" (1.5mm)

Recommended wood: ¾" (19mm) hard maple

Nestle into the vibrant jungle with this wooden puzzle. It's a snapshot of the teeming life where every creature has its place in the harmony of the wild.

Jungle Canopy
Pattern

Photocopy at 125%

Grain direction

Island Getaway

Island Getaway: 7 pieces

Size: 9⅛" x 7⅛" (230 x 180mm)

Eye sizes: ⅛" (3mm), ⁵⁄₃₂" (4mm)

Recommended wood: ¾" (19mm) hard maple

Catch some waves with this beachy wooden puzzle, where a surfer and his sea creature friends enjoy the tropical vibes under a sun-kissed palm. It's a slice of paradise for playful afternoons in the sand and surf.

Island Getaway
Pattern

Photocopy at 100%

Bugs on a Branch

Bugs on a Branch: 7 pieces

Size: 9½" x 7⅜" (241.5 x 188mm)

Eye size: ⅛" (3mm)

Detail holes: 1⁄16" (1.5mm)

Recommended wood: ¾" (19mm) hard maple

March into the miniature world with this wooden puzzle, buzzing with insects on a leafy branch. It's an adventure full of tiny tales and crawling curiosities!

Bugs on a Branch Pattern

Photocopy at 100%

Grain direction

Autumn Harvest

Autumn Harvest: 7 pieces

Size: 11" x 5¼" (279 x 134mm)

Eye size: ¹⁄₁₆" (2mm)

Detail hole: ¹⁄₁₆" (2mm)

Tire holes: ¹⁄₁₆" (2mm), ⁷⁄₃₂" (5.5mm)

Recommended wood: ¾" (19mm) hard maple

Harvest time is here! Join the farmer as he loads plump, colorful pumpkins into his trusty truck, ready for a bountiful autumn celebration.

Autumn Harvest Pattern

Photocopy at 125%

Grain direction

Grain direction

Grain direction

Bear Necessities

Bear Necessities: 9 pieces

Size: 8¹⁵⁄₁₆" x 5⅞" (227 x 150mm)

Eye sizes: ¹⁄₁₆" (2mm), ⁵⁄₃₂" (4mm)

Recommended wood: ¾" (19mm) hard maple

It's a bear-y busy fishing day by the river! Watch as this bear duo enjoys a splashy feast, hooking fish after fish in this delightful wooden scene.

Bear Necessities
Pattern

Photocopy at 100%

Grain direction

Potted Pals

Potted Pals: 6 pieces

Size: 9½" x 9" (241 x 228mm)

Eye size: ⅛" (3mm)

Detail hole: ¹⁄₁₆" (2mm)

Recommended wood: ¾" (19mm) hard maple

Climb along with the busy ants on a journey to a butterfly perched atop a potted plant. This wooden puzzle celebrates the tiny, bustling world of insects and the beauty found in the smallest gardens.

Potted Pals Pattern

Photocopy at 100%

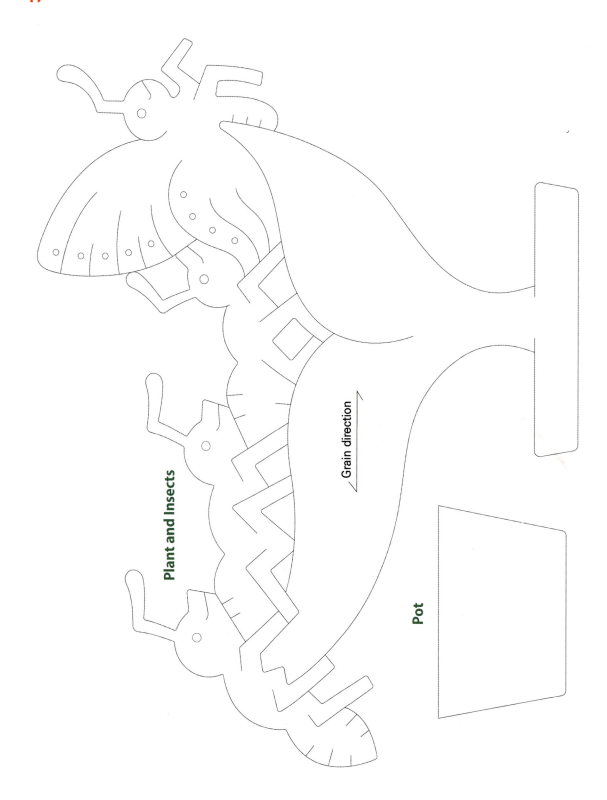

Plant and Insects

Grain direction

Pot

Mermaid Cove

Mermaid Cove: 9 pieces

Size: 10¹³⁄₁₆" x 5³⁄₁₆" (274 x 132mm)

Eye size: ¹⁄₁₆" (2mm), ⅛" (3mm), ⁵⁄₃₂" (4mm), ³⁄₁₆" (5mm)

Recommended wood: ¾" (19mm) hard maple

Dive into a whimsical underwater parade with mermaids and their sea creature friends! This colorful wooden puzzle takes you on a splashy undersea adventure.

Mermaid Cove
Pattern

Photocopy at 125%

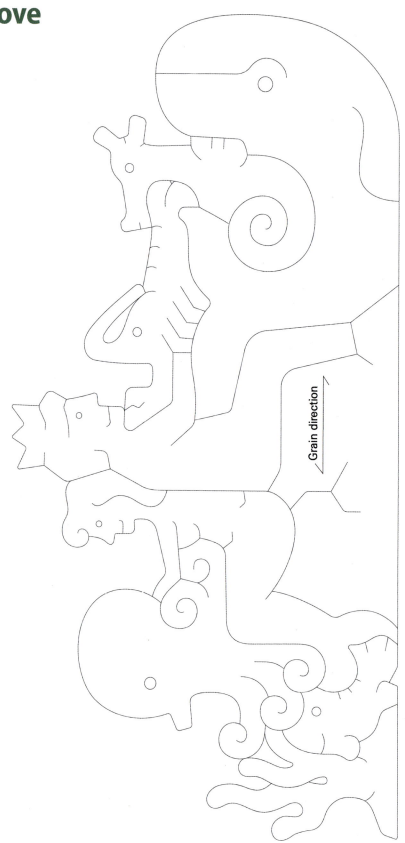

Grain direction

Frozen Tundra

Frozen Tundra: 13 pieces

Size: 10³⁄₁₆" x 7⁷⁄₁₆" (259 x 189mm)

Eye sizes: ¹⁄₁₆" (2mm), ⅛" (3mm), ³⁄₁₆" (5mm)

Recommended wood: ¾" (19mm) hard maple

Venture to wilder climes in this chilly, wintry scene! Complete with owl, buffalo, rabbit, and reindeer, this puzzle is sure to bring the magic of sweater weather right to your playroom.

Frozen Tundra
Pattern

Photocopy at 125%

Grain direction

Fantastic Frenzy

Fantastic Frenzy: 9 pieces

Size: 12¼" x 5⅜" (312 x 137mm)

Eye sizes: ¹⁄₁₆" (2mm), ⁵⁄₃₂" (4mm)

Detail hole: ¹⁄₁₆" (1.5mm)

Recommended wood: ¾" (19mm) hard maple

Conjure up a world of myth and magic with this puzzle. Create your own stories of fantastic legend and lore!

Fantastic Frenzy
Pattern (Part A)

Photocopy at 100%

Grain direction

Fantastic Frenzy
Pattern (Part B)

Photocopy at 100%

Grain direction

Grain direction

Pasture Pals

Pasture Pals : 10 pieces

Size: 10⅞" x 6¼" (277 x 158mm)

Eye size: ⅛" (3mm)

Recommended wood: ¾" (19mm) hard maple

Gather the herd with this peaceful wooden puzzle, featuring dogs and sheep enjoying the shelter of a grand tree. It's a tranquil farm scene that promises rest and camaraderie in every piece.

Pasture Pals
Pattern (Variation A)

Photocopy at 125%

Pasture Pals
Pattern (Variation B)

Photocopy at 125%

Lazy Lily Pond

Lazy Lily Pond: 8 pieces

Size: 14⅛" x 4⁵⁄₁₆" (358.5 x 110mm)

Eye size: ⁹⁄₆₄" (3.5mm)

Detail hole: ⁹⁄₆₄" (3.5mm)

Recommended wood: ¾" (19mm) hard maple

Leap into a lily pond scene where frogs and friends bask in the sun. It's a playful peek into the pond's lively dance of life and color.

Lazy Lily Pond Pattern

Photocopy at 125%

Frogs, Plants, Cat

Bug

Under Construction

Under Construction: 13 pieces

Size: 10¹⁵⁄₁₆" x 5⅞" (278 x 150mm)

Eye size: ¹⁄₁₆" (2mm)

Detail holes: ⁵⁄₃₂" (4mm), ⁹⁄₃₂" (7mm)

Recommended wood: ¾" (19mm) hard maple

Hard hats on! This construction crew is ready for action, with every worker and piece of equipment playing a part in building something great.

Under Construction
Pattern (Heavy Equipment)

Photocopy at 125%

Under Construction
Pattern (Figures)

Photocopy at 125%

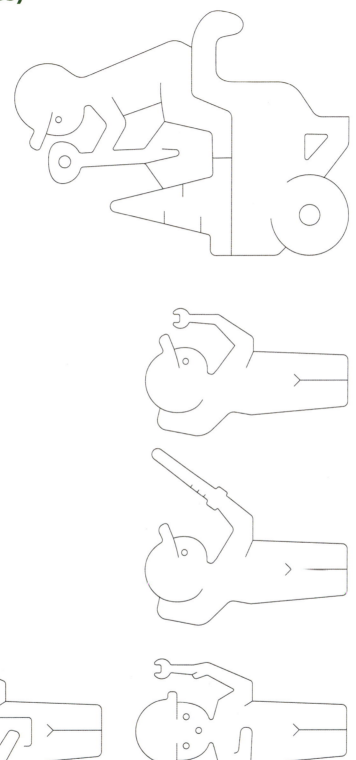

Scarecrow and Friends

Scarecrow and Friends: 6 pieces

Size: 11¼" x 6⁷⁄₁₆" (285 x 163mm)

Eye size: ⅛" (3mm)

Detail hole: ¹⁄₃₂" (1mm)

Recommended wood: ¾" (19mm) hard maple

Amidst the autumn fields, a friendly scarecrow stands guard while a cheerful worm and a spry grasshopper explore the bounties of the harvest. It's a festive celebration of the season's change, inviting you to join in the fun!

Scarecrow and Friends Pattern (Part A)

Photocopy at 100%

Grain direction

Scarecrow and Friends Pattern (Part B)

Photocopy at 100%

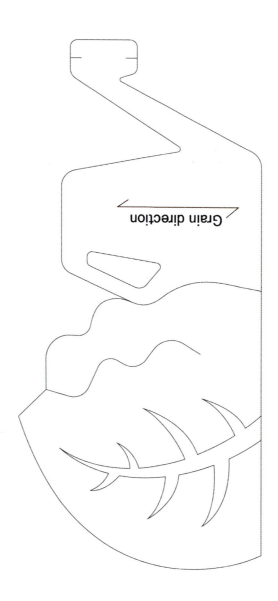

Grain direction

Deep Sea Dive

Deep Sea Dive: 6 pieces

Size: 10⅞" x 4¹⁵⁄₁₆" (277 x 125mm)

Eye size: ⅛" (3mm)

Recommended wood: ¾" (19mm) hard maple

Dive deep with this wooden puzzle to explore the ocean's wonders, from the curious creatures of the deep to the mysterious submarine that roams the silent, dark depths.

Deep Sea Dive
Pattern

Photocopy at 125%

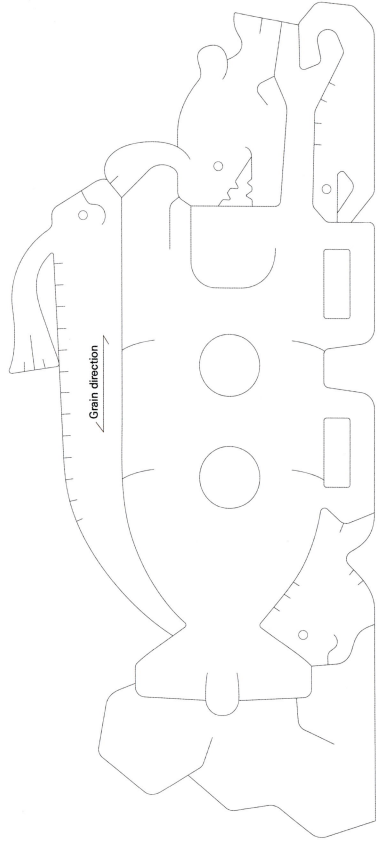

Grain direction

Shipwreck

Shipwreck: 8 pieces

Size: 11" x 5⁵⁄₁₆" (279 x 135mm)

Eye size: ⅛" (3mm)

Detail hole: ⅛" (3mm)

Recommended wood: ¾" (19mm) hard maple

Uncover a sunken story with this wooden puzzle, where the mysteries of a shipwreck come to life amidst friendly sea creatures of the deep. Each piece is a clue to the tales hidden at the ocean floor!

Shipwreck Pattern

Photocopy at 125%

Fairy Kingdom

Fairy Kingdom: 5 pieces

Size: 8¾" x 7⅛" (222mm x 180mm)

Eye sizes: ⅛" (2mm), ⅛" (3mm), ¼" (6mm)

Mushroom holes: ⅛" (3mm), 9⁄32" (7mm)

Recommended wood: ¾" (19mm) hard maple

In a secret garden, a whimsical fairy flutters by, her wings aglow with the magic of nature as she dances among flowers and toadstools. This enchanting puzzle invites you into a world where fantasy blooms.

Fairy Kingdom
Pattern

Photocopy at 100%

Grain direction

Green Thumb

Green Thumb: 10 pieces

Size: 8½" x 7¼" (216 x 185mm)

Eye size: ⅛" (3mm)

Detail holes: ⅛" (3mm), ³⁄₁₆" (5mm)

Recommended wood: ¾" (19mm) hard maple

Get ready to dig in and grow with this garden-themed puzzle, where a wheelbarrow full of vibrant plants and trusty tools awaits the joy of gardening. It's a tribute to the green thumb in all of us!

Green Thumb
Pattern

Photocopy at 100%

Grain direction

Sweet Treats

Sweet Treats: 11 pieces

Size: 7¾" x 7½" (197 x 190mm)

Donut hole: ¹⁄₁₆" (1.5mm)

Recommended wood: ¾" (19mm) hard maple

Indulge in a sweet assortment with this delectable puzzle, featuring a doughnut, ice cream, and other treats that look almost good enough to eat. It's a delightful way to enjoy dessert without the calories.

Sweet Treats
Pattern

Photocopy at 100%

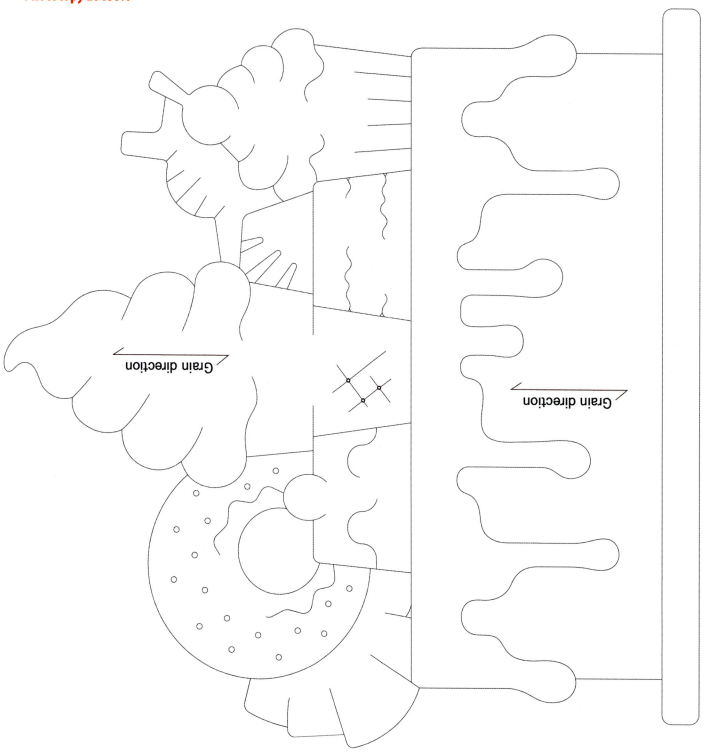

Tools of the Trade

Tools of the Trade: 10 pieces

Size: 16⅜" x 7¼" (416 x 185mm)

Detail holes: ⅛" (3mm), ³⁄₁₆" (5mm), ¼" (6mm)

Recommended wood: ¾" (19mm) hard maple

Gear up with this wooden puzzle, a carpenter's delight, full of hand tools and power tools ready to create and fix. Each piece fits together to build the ultimate toolbox for any craft or project.

Tools of the Trade
Pattern (Set A)

Photocopy at 125%

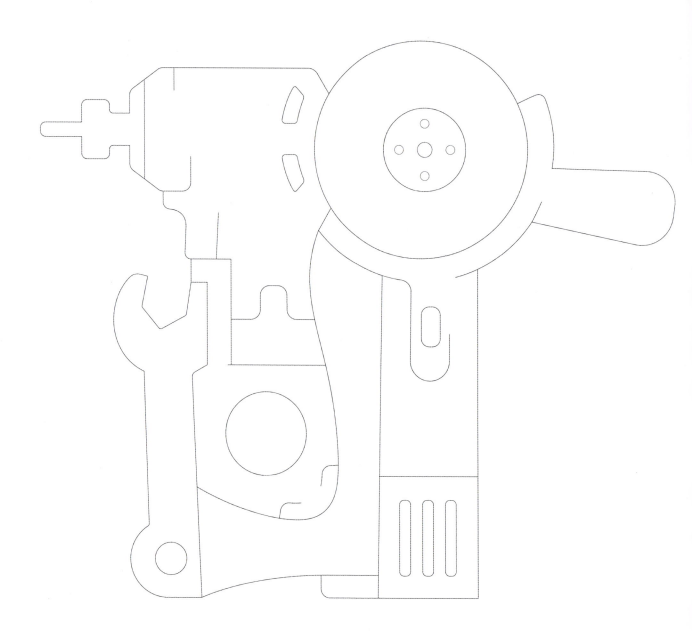

Tools of the Trade
Pattern (Set B)

Photocopy at 125%

Index

Use your imagination to make each piece uniquely your own and create endless hours of fun and adventure for the whole family.